D1283241

SUSAN B. ANTHONY

A Crusader for Women's Rights

BY BARBARA SALSINI

B. S. Marquette Univ Col. of Journalism

SamHar Press

Division of Story House Corp.

D. Steve Rahmas, *A. B., J. D., Columbia U., Editor*

Compiled with the assistance of the Research Staff of SamHar Press.

SamHar Press
Charlotteville, N.Y.   12036
A Division of Story House Corp.

1973

(The above card has been cataloged by the editor and may not be
identical to that of Library of Congress. Library card portrayed above
is 80% of original size.)

14935

SUSAN B. ANTHONY

A Crusader for Women's Rights

In 1872, Susan B. Anthony shocked the nation with an unpardonable breach of etiquette. She voted. For this unladylike offense, she was arrested, found guilty and fined $100. She never paid the fine, but even if she had been forced to do so, it would have represented only a tiny fraction of the total price women paid for the precious privilege of voting.

While Miss Anthony's rebellion inspired many thoughtful Americans, still others were outraged by her "brazen" presumption. The next thing they knew, it was grumbled, she and her followers would be wanting equal pay for equal work, coeducational schools and indecent clothes like those shocking Bloomer outfits. Didn't Miss Anthony and all those suffragettes know that women were too refined and pure for such worldly pursuits, that a woman's place was in the home?

Susan B. Anthony was neither a brazen woman nor the hardboiled spinster that cartoonists loved to caricature. To her young followers, she was "Aunt Susan," and more than one man wanted to marry her. As her cause grew more respectable, even anti-feminists warmed to the determined Miss Anthony. So regularly did she appear in Washington to lobby for her cause that, it was noted, the sight of her famous red shawl was a sure sign of spring in the capitol.

For more than fifty years, Susan B. Anthony carried her message of woman's rights to an audience often full of hostile men and--far worse--apathetic women. At her side was Elizabeth Cady Stanton, who had started the movement by demanding the right to vote at the historic Seneca Falls Woman's Rights Convention in 1848. So close was their partnership that it was sometimes said Mrs. Stanton shaped the bullets and her accomplice fired them. Despite the grueling work of this great suffrage team and other women's rights pioneers, it was not until 1920 that the Nineteenth Amendment gave American women the right to vote. Susan B. Anthony did not live to see this dream come true and probably would have had little patience with many modern women who treat this privilege so lightly that they often neglect to vote.

This most liberated of American women was born on February 15, 1820, near Adams, Massachusetts, where her father, Daniel, was a cotton manufacturer. She was named Susan Brownell, after an aunt. From girlhood Susan admired her father, whose integrity and high moral principles she maintained in her own life. Another lasting influence on the future reformer was her family's Quaker heritage, a tradition that not only stressed humanitarian values but also gave women a much greater role than did most other religions.

Although Daniel Anthony was an upright Quaker, he did not automatically conform to any standards but instead acted out of his own convictions. Reprimanded for selling liquor at a store in his home, he not only stopped this practice but became a temperance advocate. On the other hand, when he was criticized for wearing a cloak that was judged too flamboyant for the austere Quaker style, he continued to wear the offensive garment.

The most significant result of this independent thinking was his marriage to Lucy Read, one of his pupils in the school his father had established. Because Lucy was not a Quaker, there were objections to the union. But Daniel would not give up the fun-loving girl and even permitted her to have one last fling. Because marriage to a Quaker ruled out such frolicking, Lucy danced until four o'clock in the morning while Daniel watched from the sidelines.

Lucy Anthony must often have recalled that gay evening during the exhausting years that followed. Though her life was no harder than that of other women in her circumstances and, blessed with an understanding husband, may even have been easier, the routine of the nineteenth century housewife was almost overwhelming. Childbirth was dangerous, but large families were common. Lucy Anthony was more fortunate than many of her contemporaries, for of the eight children she bore, six lived to maturity. First came Guelma, then Susan, Hannah, Daniel, Mary and Merritt. It was a close knit family and remained so even after the children had homes and families of their own, and, in Susan's case, great causes.

In 1826, Daniel Anthony moved his family forty-four miles to Battenville, New York, where he had been offered a partnership in a cotton factory. His new business flourished, and he built a fine brick house. In Battenville, Susan had her first glimpse of the system of slavery that was to claim so much of her energy in the future.

Susan first attended the local district school. Her ambition to learn long division was thwarted by the schoolmaster who thought it ridiculous for a girl to want to learn such an unnecessary subject--perhaps because he apparently had not mastered the skill himself. Fortunately for the Anthony girls, their father's enlightened philosophy extended to education, and he wanted them, as well as his sons, to have good schooling. Accordingly, he set up his own school and tried to hire good teachers. They were not, however, permitted to teach singing, a practice ruled too frivolous for Quakers. He also provided evening classes for millworkers and used the schoolroom for worship services.

Like many Quakers, Daniel Anthony did not vote and was opposed to paying taxes. It was hard to avoid the latter, however, so he would deposit his pocketbook in front of the tax collector and let that official appropriate the required sum. He maintained his opposition to liquor and slavery even when such views threatened his livelihood. It was expected that liquor would be available at the company store and during the construction of company housing, but he refused to provide it. The morality of using slave-produced cotton was a dilemma for opponents of slavery, but Daniel eased his conscience by trying to buy cotton that was not produced by slave labor.

From visits to her father's mill, Susan gained an early insight into the unequal status of women. Not only did the busy millgirls work for a mere $1.50 a week, but one of the women was obviously more capable than the male overseer. When one of the mill workers became ill, Susan and her sister Hannah begged to take the sick woman's place temporarily. Susan drew the winning straw, promising to split her wages with Hannah. After two weeks, she had earned three dollars and spent her share on china dishes for her mother.

Susan began her teaching career when she was fifteen years old, first working in the home school. Her sisters also taught, raising the eyebrows of some neighbors who thought it improper for the daughters of a prosperous man like Daniel Anthony to work. At the age of seventeen, Susan was enrolled at Deborah Moulson's Friends' Seminary, a girls' boarding school near Philadelphia. Her sister Guelma had studied there the previous year and was now on the teaching staff. The cost for a year's education, including board, was $125.

The year at the school was a trying time for Susan. She enjoyed science and algebra but, in the school's repressive atmosphere, agonized over innocent "moral" failings. She tried hard to improve herself and win Miss Moulson's approval. In one such attempt, she was clearing cobwebs off the schoolroom ceiling when she stepped on the principal's desk and damaged it. Many years later she could not remember the humiliating incident without pain.

A financial depression set in at this time, and Daniel Anthony's business failed. A boarding school venture in his home also proved unprofitable, especially when four of the students were discovered playing cards and were sent home in disgrace. Back from Philadelphia, Susan returned to teaching, contributing her earnings to the family budget. But hard times continued and, in 1839, the Anthonys were forced to give up their home. Everything, from clothing to food in the larder, was put up for sale. Susan managed to rescue some of the family belongings with $11 she had saved, while a generous uncle, Joshua Read, salvaged a larger share.

With their depleted furnishings the family moved a short distance to Hardscrabble, later called Center Falls. Here Daniel still owned two small, unfortunately mortgaged, mills. Their new home had once been a tavern, and Mrs. Anthony augmented their meager income by again opening the house to travelers. When Daniel was named postmaster of Center Falls, the Anthonys were permitted to mail letters without paying postage--a welcome bonus for them.

When Susan's teaching duties were over, she helped at home. One day, she recorded in her diary, she baked twenty-one loaves of bread, washed clothes and put in a stint at the spinning wheel. On the previous day she had woven three yards of carpet.

For a few months in 1839 Susan taught at a Quaker girls' school in New Rochelle, New York. She later recalled being disturbed one day when three black girls, visiting the Quaker meeting, were given seats in the gallery. She tried to make up for this insulting treatment by inviting the girls to tea. She had equally strong views on drinking. When President Martin Van Buren was in the neighborhood, she refused to go to see him, ostensibly because the President was reported to enjoy wine and the theater. In New Rochelle, she was impressed by a Quaker woman preacher and observed that it was ridiculous to confine women to the domestic sphere.

Once, when Susan was in charge, relatives of a pupil put in an appearance at the school. Told that their child had been punished by being sent to bed, they upbraided Susan, reducing her to tears. She was not yet used to the hostility or disapproval that would become all too familiar in the future.

Susan returned home for the marriage of her sister and taught in a local school. She attracted her own share of suitors and received her first marriage proposal. She turned down the proposal as she later did that of a prosperous Quaker who told Susan she brought back the memory of his first wife--hardly a tactful argument. Obviously Susan was not unattractive despite an annoying eye defect about which she was unnecessarily self-conscious. An operation to correct the condition proved a failure.

While in Center Falls, the strongminded Daniel Anthony again became embroiled in trouble with Quaker leaders. The Anthony home had a ballroom on its upper floor, dating from the days when the house had been a tavern. Now some of the area's young people wanted to use it. At first Daniel refused, since dancing was against Quaker rules. But when he learned that the alternative gathering place was a tavern that served liquor, he agreed to the proposal. Susan and her sisters were allowed to go up and watch the dancing, provided they did not participate in this forbidden pleasure. The Quakers did not agree with Daniel's reasoning and disowned him. He was saddened by the decision against him but felt that his "offense" had been the most virtuous action of his life.

Daniel's financial difficulties continued. Susan's contribution of her $2.50 weekly teaching salary helped but could not save him. (It must have been galling for her to realize that male teachers earned four times as much.) Deciding to make a fresh start, Daniel bought a thirty-two acre farm near Rochester, New York. Money for the purchase came from his wife's inheritance. Since at that time a married woman could not legally own property and the inheritance could have been seized by Daniel's creditors if he had claimed it, the money was being kept for Lucy by her brother, Joshua Read.

After they arrived at their new home that cold autumn night in 1845, Lucy Anthony warmed her family with a pot of cornmeal mush. It was not a good time of year to start farming, and Daniel returned to teaching temporarily, earning $10 a week. He soon made friends among some of Rochester's Quaker citizens who welcomed such an intelligent newcomer.

The problem of Susan's immediate future was solved with the help of her Uncle Joshua. He was the trustee of an academy at Canajoharie, New York, and suggested that Susan be hired as headmistress of the "female department." Her salary was $110 a year, out of which she paid $45 for lodgings at the home of a cousin.

At Canajoharie, Susan blossomed into a fashionable young woman. Apparently she had lost much of her earlier primness, but she still preferred that her escorts be teetotalers. With her father's financial affairs improving, she was free to spend money on herself, paying $22.50 for a shawl and $30 for a mantilla. She must have looked fetching in the new straw hat that was decked out with fringed white ribbon, a pink stripe, white roses and green leaves. On examination day, she wore her hair braided and arranged with a shell comb and was so attractive in her plaid gown and patent leather shoes that there were predictions that some infatuated swain would carry her away.

Elected president of the Canajoharie chapter of the Daughters of Temperance, Susan gave her first public speech in 1849 at a fund-raising event. The speech, recorded in a manuscript sewn together and topped with a blue cover, reminded women that they could discourage drinking by showing their disapproval. It was well received; the triumphant orator received a bouquet and saw her name spelled out in evergreens as part of the decorations.

After three years she left Canajoharie and returned to Rochester to find the Quakers there split on the slavery issue. Daniel belonged to the group that favored prompt emancipation. When the famous Unitarian preacher, William Henry Channing, arrived in Rochester, this group and the Anthony family began attending his church.

Fortunately, Daniel Anthony was back on the road to prosperity, this time in the life insurance business. On her return to Rochester, Susan helped manage the farm to free him for his insurance work and also did some teaching, retiring from her "schoolmarm" career in the early 1850's. She continued her interest in the Daughters of Temperance as president of the Rochester group.

Now in her thirties, she was still not clear what direction her life would take. Her father's example must have led her to demand a great deal of herself, and the turbulent times demanded even more. Without leaving her home, she could meet some of the outstanding reformers of her day when they visited Daniel Anthony. Among his guests were the former slave, Frederick Douglass, who published a newspaper in Rochester, and the legendary abolitionists William Lloyd Garrison and Wendell Phillips. Sometimes she helped cook for twenty guests, hurrying between the kitchen and the dining room in order not to miss the stimulating discussions. She also spent a memorable week touring with the inspiring anti-slavery orator, Abby Kelley Foster.

Besides temperance and abolition, another reform was in the air during those heady days of the 1850's. This movement, opposed even by some who approved the other two reforms, was a drive for women's rights. Susan was not present at the first women's rights convention at Seneca Falls, New York, in 1848, and was apparently among the majority who regarded the affair as a laughing matter. But members of her family attended a second convention held in Rochester and were impressed by the women's demands. Susan was intrigued. The Seneca Falls Woman's Rights Convention was a landmark in the history of American feminism. At its helm was Elizabeth Cady Stanton, the dynamic woman who would become Susan B. Anthony's closest friend and ally in the crusade for women's rights.

Five years older than Susan, Mrs. Stanton had a more genteel background, being the daughter of a judge in Johnstown, New York. The disadvantages of womanhood were brought home to her when she heard women complaining to her father about laws that favored their husbands. These women were not objecting to laws that denied their right to vote--as Susan and Mrs. Stanton were to do so effectively--but about rules that denied or limited their rights over their property and children. On a personal level, Mrs. Stanton had suffered as a girl because her father did not respect her high achievements as he would have honored those of a son.

Her marriage to Henry Stanton in 1840 brought Elizabeth into the stimulating world of the anti-slavery movement. Stanton was an anti-slavery orator. Immediately after the wedding, he and his bride traveled to England where he was an American delegate to the World Anti-Slavery Convention. In London, the young Mrs. Stanton met Lucretia Mott, the Quaker preacher whose refined presence lent dignity to the anti-slavery and feminist movements. Although Mrs. Mott and other American women had been appointed delegates to the convention, male opposition banished them to a gallery where they were joined by the sympathetic William Lloyd Garrison. Mrs. Mott and Mrs. Stanton were incensed by this flagrant example of male chauvinism on the part of those preaching racial justice. Clearly it was time to act on behalf of women, and the pair decided to call a women's rights convention at a future date in America.

For the next eight years, the young matron was busy with her growing family, but in 1848 she and Mrs. Mott were able to fulfill the promise made in London. With three other women, they planned the Seneca Falls Woman's Rights Convention, never dreaming that it would become a momentous event in American history and the start of a long crusade for women's suffrage.

About three hundred people--male and female-- showed up at the long delayed convention and heard a Declaration of Sentiments, patterned after the Declaration of Independence. Women's grievances were outlined and resolutions for reform proposed, the most daring being Elizabeth Stanton's challenge that women gain their right to vote. Many of those present felt that this was going too far, and even Lucretia Mott was afraid the introduction of such a farfetched subject as women's suffrage would make them seem "ridiculous."

Among those present at the meeting was Amelia Bloomer, publisher of a temperance newspaper to which Mrs. Stanton contributed. She is best remembered for the bizarre costume that bears her name; it was actually designed by Mrs. Stanton's cousin, Elizabeth Smith Miller, but Mrs. Bloomer became identified with it after she publicized the outfit in her paper. Like Mrs. Stanton's demand for the vote, the Bloomer was regarded as an outrage, for it showed that women had those most unmentionable features, legs (known as "limbs" in polite society). In the opinion of its wearers, the Bloomer was more than just a comfortable style or fashion fad, for it freed them from the cumbersome gowns that symbolized their constricting lives. Its most striking feature was a pair of baggy trousers, worn under a knee-length dress. Ludicrously modest by modern standards, the Bloomer shocked the more innocent eyes of the Victorian age. Typically, Mrs. Stanton was one of the first to don the costume, to the dismay of her son, who begged her not to visit his school while thus adorned.

The paths of Susan B. Anthony and Elizabeth Cady Stanton first crossed in 1851. The busy Mrs. Bloomer provided the introduction--a more significant claim to fame for Amelia Bloomer than her notorious fashion namesake. Susan had gone to Seneca Falls for an anti-slavery meeting and met Mrs. Stanton on a street-corner, the former in demure gray, the latter in her Bloomers. Preoccupied at the moment, Mrs. Stanton did not invite Susan to dinner that day but said later that she had liked her at first sight.

Their friendship deepened that summer when Susan went to Seneca Falls to consult with Mrs. Stanton, editor Horace Greeley and feminist Lucy Stone about a proposed coeducational college. The meeting, otherwise unprofitable, brought Susan into contact with Lucy Stone, a woman ranked with the Anthony-Stanton team as one of the heroines of American feminism. Among the first woman college graduates in the United States, Lucy married Henry Blackwell, brother of America's first woman doctor. Despite more enduring contributions to the women's rights movement, Lucy Stone is remembered chiefly for her refusal to change her name after she married.

They were only a handful, these pioneer feminists, but as the first on a stage that women had previously shunned, they had an impact far beyond their numbers. Other early arrivals in the public arena were Ernestine Rose, Paulina Wright Davis, Abby Kelley Foster, Lucretia Mott and the Grimke sisters of South Carolina. Another of Susan's contemporaries was Antoinette

Brown Blackwell, America's first ordained woman minister and wife of a second Blackwell brother. A personal favorite of Susan's was Anna Dickinson, a spectacularly successful orator of the Civil War era. Other prominent women of the day were Dr. Elizabeth Blackwell, Julia Ward Howe, who wrote the words of "The Battle Hymn of the Republic," and Harriett Beecher Stowe, author of *Uncle Tom's Cabin*. While not all notable women of the time were ardent feminists, they nonetheless helped the cause by drawing attention to woman's potential.

Many feminists came to the movement through the anti-slavery crusade. Speaking out against slavery, they not only gained confidence in their abilities but also found similarities between racial injustice and their own subservient position in a male-oriented society. Others, like Susan B. Anthony, first served the temperance cause. Because women were deemed the chief victims of male alcoholism, temperance was often allied with feminism. Despite the sympathy of many male reformers, women who worked in the temperance and anti-slavery fields sometimes encountered sexual prejudice even within the movements and thus were pushed into feminism. In much the same way, a century later, many women involved in civil rights and peace activities complained that they were automatically appointed coffee makers and envelope stuffers while men took over the executive positions.

Just how valid was their complaint? Were American women really given no more legal rights than criminals and lunatics? Some historians have pointed out that individual laws and common usage gave women more rights than was sometimes claimed. Of course, women have often played dominant roles in home life, and there have always been outstanding women to serve as examples for the rest of the sex. However, guardianship and property laws favored the man of the family. In the most flagrant instances of injustice allowable under the laws, a husband could usurp his wife's wages and property or take away her children.

Such cases were rare, but women were truly second class citizens in the economic and political spheres.

Centuries of tradition had pinned them to a small orbit and held them in "their place." They were not permitted to vote although they were citizens; they were "taxed without representation"; they faced a male jury, not their "peers," when brought to trial.

To make up for these drawbacks, women were placed on pedestals and told that their role was a spiritual one, to elevate man to high ideals. Even many feminists were influenced by this view and promised that when women got the vote their loftier standards would raise the moral stature of the nation. They have been accused of contradicting themselves by simultaneously claiming equality and feminine superiority.

Women who deviated from the norm were regarded with disapproval. Girls showing tomboy tendencies were dubbed "Susan B's," after the infamous Miss Anthony. Under such conditions, it took great courage for most women to appear on public platforms. Unaccustomed to the spotlight, they first had to conquer stagefright and learn how to strengthen their trembling voices. Mrs. Stanton was adept at speaking and writing, while Susan found both an ordeal. Among her special gifts were organizational ability, discipline and unyielding dedication to her cause. Support from members of her family meant a great deal to Susan. A more typical attitude was that of one brother-in-law. A woman who could bake biscuits as tasty as Susan's, he teased, was more to his liking than one who knew algebra. Susan pointed out that the same woman could acquire both skills.

In 1848, the year of the Seneca Falls convention, women received another boost with the passage of a Married Women's Property Law in New York. Elizabeth Stanton and other women had urged the adoption of this legislation, but its passage was due largely to the efforts of New Yorkers who wanted to preserve family holdings. The law gave married women the right to own property, which meant that Mrs. Anthony could now claim the inheritance that had been held for her in the name of her brother. For determined feminists, the law was a spur to further action.

Much of the early strategy for the women's rights

movement was mapped in Mrs. Stanton's house in Seneca Falls where, amid the clatter of toddlers and household routine, its mistress and Susan Anthony plotted their campaigns. The two complemented each other so well that it is now difficult to assess the achievement of one without that of the other. As a housewife and mother, Mrs. Stanton was more restricted than her partner, so the former supplied much of the movement's philosophy while the latter did the leg work. When Susan arrived in Seneca Falls, it was with a "portmanteau" crammed with a horrifying array of woman's grievances, "injustice enough to turn any woman's thoughts from stockings and puddings," according to Mrs. Stanton. They would indignantly take up pens to write petitions, protests, articles, letters and resolutions, meanwhile keeping order on the domestic front where the exuberant Stanton children presented another formidable challenge.

The two friends often disagreed in private, but outwardly they showed a united front. Susan glorified in Mrs. Stanton's talents and did not mind being overshadowed by her in public. She continued to call the older woman "Mrs. Stanton," to whom she was "Susan." When feminists temporarily deserted the cause for such a mundane reason as pregnancy, Susan was dismayed. She complained to Mrs. Stanton: "Those of you who have the talent to do honor to poor--oh! how poor--womanhood, have all given yourselves over to baby-making; and left poor brainless me to do battle alone." One year their annual convention was not held because too many feminist leaders had conceded to maternity. Susan might have been comforted had she known that some of those babies would continue the crusade, among them Alice Stone Blackwell and Harriot Stanton Blatch.

For a time in the 1850's, Susan continued her activities in support of temperance. It was at a meeting of a men's temperance group that she received the now famous rebuff: "the sisters were not invited there to speak but to listen and learn." Susan and several others left the meeting and called another one at which it was decided to sponsor a women's temperance convention.

Mrs. Stanton and Susan held the offices of president and secretary in the new Woman's State Temperance Society, but when men gained influence in the organization, Mrs. Stanton lost her office and they both resigned.

Attending a teacher's convention in 1853, Susan listened to male teachers bemoan the low prestige of their profession. After waiting half an hour before being permitted to speak, she asked, "Do you not see that so long as society says a woman is incompetent to be a lawyer, minister, or doctor, but has ample ability to be a teacher, that every man of you who chooses this profession tacitly acknowledges that he has no more brains than a woman?" At another teacher's meeting, Susan spoke on the subject of coeducation. One male listener complimented her on the speech but said he would rather have his wife and daughter dead and buried than follow her example.

With true heroism, Susan followed those fervent feminists who had put on the Bloomer costume. The style was not made for her angular dimensions and it was agony for her to appear in it, no matter how much more comfortable it was than the conventional styles of the day. A woman speaker was unusual enough in the 1850's, but a woman in Bloomers was the delight of every heckler. Following Mrs. Stanton's example and advice, Susan let down her hems after wearing the costume for about a year, and the Bloomer craze fizzled out. How gratified its champions would have been if they could have seen the variety of "pants" styles worn by their liberated great-granddaughters.

Without their Bloomers, the feminists again looked like ordinary women, something they most emphatically were not. Educationally, socially and culturally, they were far above the national average, and most of them were married. Mrs. Stanton was a motherly type who reeked of respectability despite her unorthodox views. People who came to see Susan expecting to find a mannish old maid were disappointed to discover that she was a lady after all.

Susan's first concentrated effort on behalf of women was a campaign to persuade the New York legislature to broaden the rights granted women by the 1848 law. But the 1854 legislators were no more moved by the thousands of signatures that had been collected on petitions than they were by Mrs. Stanton's eloquent speech. Braving the frigid New York weather in 1855, Susan lectured in fifty-four New York counties. She was her own campaign manager, arranging meeting places and buying candles to light up the gatherings. But it took more than candles to enlighten even well-meaning listeners; perhaps the main challenge to feminism, or any reform, was to change attitudes based on years of tradition. Traveling was arduous, and Susan was briefly pampered when an admiring Quaker gentleman chauffeured her in his sleigh. They parted ways after she turned down his offer of marriage, not the last such bid she was to receive. In her memoirs, Mrs. Stanton recalled that Susan liked to joke that she remained a spinster because she could not tie any man she loved to a "political slave and pariah." A sense of humor was another asset of this feminist team.

On another tour, Susan stayed at a tavern where the proprietress was a busy young wife with a baby. The woman provided comfortable accommodations for the travelers, yet when they paid their bill, her "dolt of a husband took the money and put it in his pocket." Incidents like this made Susan realize that women could not be free until they had "purses of their own." This economic dependence was brought home to her constantly by the chronic poverty of the suffrage movement. Deprived of incomes, even loyal supporters could not contribute greatly to the cause. Susan recognized that the hospitality she often received from these women was another kind of contribution.

After such rugged campaigning, it was disheartening when the New York Senate treated woman's rights as a laughing matter. Actually it was the male of the sex who should be pitied, a committee reported; women got the choicest food and treatment, their clothes cost more, and, "with the prevailing fashion one lady occupies three times as much space in the world as a gentleman." However, a law giving women broader rights was passed in 1860. It was considered a victory for the feminists and a model for other states, although part of the law was subsequently amended.

A staunch abolitionist, Susan became an agent for the American Anti-Slavery Society in 1856, arranging tours and lecturing on what was an inflammatory topic. Paid only $10 a week, plus expenses, she still wore her Canajoharie wardrobe, now remodeled and dyed. She spent little money on herself and dug into her own purse when feminist funds were low.

"Is there not something very touching in the fact that she never bought a book or picture for her own enjoyment?" asked Mrs. Stanton in her charming memoirs. She recalled four instances of Susan's "extravagance"--when she bought two modestly priced brooches, a watch, and cuffs to match a lace collar. Mrs. Stanton continued: "Those interested in Miss Anthony's personal appearance long ago ceased to trust her with the purchase-money for any ornament; for, however firm her resolution to comply with their wish, the check invariably found its way to the credit column of those little cash-books as 'money received for the cause'."

When the radical abolitionist John Brown was executed after his Harpers Ferry raid, Susan organized a memorial service in Rochester. (Previously her brother Merritt had fought with Brown in Kansas.) As war fervor grew, abolition meetings became increasingly frenzied and even dangerous. Mobs sometimes broke up the meetings, Susan's effigy was burned in Syracuse, and the mayor of Albany kept "law and order" in his city by appearing on the platform with a gun.

In the midst of her anti-slavery work, Susan maintained her concern for the women's cause, which had been bolstered by two gifts from wealthy donors in the late 1850's. At the national Woman's Rights Convention in 1860, she and Mrs. Stanton stirred controversy by their support of liberalized divorce laws. Susan was chided by a clergyman for participating in the discussion on marriage when she herself was a spinster. "Well, Mr. Mayo," was the reply. "You are not a slave. Suppose you quit lecturing on slavery."

Susan backed up her conviction with action when the wife of a prominent Massachusetts man came to her for help. The woman claimed that her husband had sent her to an insane asylum after she accused him of infidelity. The unhappy woman had been released after more than a year in confinement, but now her husband retained custody of their children. Fearlessly, Susan Anthony escorted the woman and her daughter to New York and found them a hiding place. Threats of legal action against Susan were not carried out, but the child was eventually discovered and returned to her father. Susan was distressed by the lack of support she received from her heroes, Wendell Phillips and William Lloyd Garrison. Urging her to avoid trouble, Garrison reminded her that the father had the law in his favor. Susan was not to be cautioned.

"Does not the law of the United States give the slaveholder the ownership of the slave? And don't you break it every time you help a slave to Canada?" she asked him. When Garrison agreed that this was the case, she explained, "Well, the law which gives the father the sole ownership of the children is just as wicked and I'll break it just as quickly. You would die before you would deliver a slave to his master, and I will die before I will give up that child to its father."

When the Civil War erupted, Susan returned to her family in Rochester, throwing herself into work on the farm while trying to fit the conflict into the framework of her Quaker principles. She favored immediate emancipation of the slaves and did not believe President Lincoln was proceeding fast enough in that direction. For the most part, work in the women's rights movement was suspended during the war. But the doors the war opened to women on many fronts furthered the feminist cause as much as years of propaganda.

Moving to New York City, Susan boarded with the Stantons, who had left Seneca Falls. Putting their heads together, the two partners organized the Woman's National Loyal League with Mrs. Stanton and Susan again in president-secretary positions. The League's chief activity was the circulation of petitions calling for an end to slavery. As its sole employee, Susan had to live frugally, spending thirteen cents on a midday meal of tea rusks, strawberries and milk. In order to meet expenses, each woman who signed a petition was asked to donate a penny. These tiny offerings added $3,000 to League coffers.

With the Thirteenth Amendment, abolishing slavery, near passage, the League had fulfilled its function. In 1865 Susan accepted an offer from her brother Daniel to join his family in Kansas. A prominent figure in Leavenworth, he suggested that she help edit the newspaper he published. However, he frowned on her attempts to inject racial and women's issues into the paper. Eventually she lectured her way back East where the women's movement had encountered another roadblock.

In 1866, at the first postwar Woman's Rights Convention, the American Equal Rights Association was formed to promote the rights of both women and Negroes. But suddenly the men who had once been so sympathetic to woman suffrage balked. "This is the Negro's hour," the women were told; they must wait patiently until the black man safely had the vote before demanding it for themselves. Susan replied that she would sever her right hand before agreeing to such a proposition. It seemed incredible that women who had worked so hard on behalf of the slave should still be treated like second class citizens. And all those black women who had been freed--were they now to be denied the full rights of citizenship? It was an agonizing time for the feminists. Many, like Lucy Stone, agreed reluctantly that the Negro had priority. Others, led by Susan and Mrs. Stanton, insisted that simple justice demanded equal treatment, and that women should be enfranchised with the former slaves. It was only human if some of these educated, accomplished women resented being preceded in the voting booth by a group of men largely illiterate and unprepared for citizenship.

One of the bestknown incidents in the Anthony-Stanton career occurred at the New York Constitutional Convention in 1867. As the partners were being questioned, Horace Greeley asked: "Ladies, you will please remember that the bullet and ballot go together. If you vote, are you ready to fight?" The reply was: "We are ready to fight, sir, just as you fought in the late war, by sending substitutes." Greeley was further embarrassed later in the convention when a suffrage petition, bearing his wife's name on top, was offered just as he was scheduled to present a report. The editor was so incensed that he called Susan and Mrs. Stanton "about the best maneuverers among the New York politicians" and threatened to ignore their cause in his important *Tribune*.

With Kansas citizens about to vote on woman and Negro suffrage, Susan, Mrs. Stanton and other suffragists invaded the state in 1867. Their campaign was not for the faint-hearted: lodgings were wretched, food was worse, transportation ranged from mule team to lumber wagon and, as Mrs. Stanton recalled, "nights were miserable, owing to the general opinion among pioneers that a certain species of insect must necessarily perambulate the beds in a young civilization." In addition to speaking, Susan sold tracts, arranged for halls and publicity and sometimes wielded a broom and dust pan. Such zeal was not enough to move Kansas voters, and both Negro and woman suffrage were rejected.

The unsuccessful Kansas foray introduced the Anthony-Stanton team to a man who would leave a vivid mark on the women's rights movement. George Francis Train, a dapper if eccentric sympathizer, joined the Kansas campaign on behalf of woman suffrage. It was hoped that Train, a Democrat, would help the suffrage cause among Democratic voters, and Susan learned to appreciate this unconventional companion as they worked together in Kansas. But the collaboration with Train alienated many otherwise disposed toward women's rights; they were skeptical about his financial philosophy, what was considered his bigoted attitude toward Negroes, and his presidential candidacy. In the eyes of Susan and Mrs. Stanton, these drawbacks were balanced by Train's views on woman suffrage, so they accepted his offer of financial help for a suffrage newspaper and for a luxurious lecture tour on the way home from Kansas.

The paper, with the apt name of *The Revolution*, began publication in January, 1868. A weekly, its editors were Mrs. Stanton and Parker Pillsbury, with Susan as manager. Train, however, was soon under arrest in Ireland for another of his causes, and his financial support dwindled. Besides woman suffrage, *The Revolution* tackled such issues as sexual prejudice, prostitution, educated suffrage, economics, workingwomen's problems, marriage and divorce. Some of these topics were controversial, and critics felt that they diverted attention from the main issue of suffrage.

Managing *The Revolution* must have been a full-time job, but Susan also found time to organize women laborers and become president of the Workingwoman's Central Association. When she spoke to these women, she made clear that they could not expect great economic gains until they had the vote. Her desire to help them led her to suggest that women enter the printing trade during a printers' strike. This led labor leaders to call her a strikebreaker, thus diminishing her influence in the labor movement.

Meanwhile, the women's rights movement was undergoing a crisis, with reformers disagreeing on methods and goals. The more conservative element had yielded to the "Negro first" argument, while the more liberal group, led by Susan and Mrs. Stanton, rejected it. Other sore spots resulted from the Train episode and Mrs. Stanton's "radical" views on educated suffrage, marriage and religion.

The convention of the American Equal Rights Association in 1869 brought the split into the open with criticism of *The Revolution* and Train and of Susan's handling of organization funds. A vote of confidence in Susan followed this rebuke. More important was the convention's endorsement of the Fifteenth Amendment. This measure gave the vote to former slaves, made citizens by the Fourteenth Amendment, but granted suffrage only to males.

Quickly breaking away from their longtime allies in what many viewed as irregular and highhanded proceedings, Susan and Mrs. Stanton formed the National

Woman Suffrage Association. A short time later, Lucy Stone's group organized the American Woman Suffrage Association. Susan attended the first meeting of the rival group, and for a time there was hope of cooperation and reunion. But while the factions often worked for the same reforms, they were not reconciled for many years.

The goal of both groups was woman suffrage, but they disagreed on the best way to achieve it. The National leaders believed they should pressure Congress for a Sixteenth Amendment to enfranchise women and were pleased when such an amendment was proposed to Congress in 1869. In time the suffrage measure was called the "Susan B. Anthony Amendment." The American Association strategists thought it best to work within individual states, attempting to win suffrage on a state level. While Susan and Mrs. Stanton also worked hard in these campaigns, they made Washington their main focus and held yearly conventions in that city. Years later, when a reunified suffrage organization scheduled Washington conventions only in alternate years, Susan considered the move a mistake.

The rift between the two groups deepened when the National group allied themselves with the extraordinary Victoria C. Woodhull. Beautiful, charming, but with a cloudy past, Mrs. Woodhull had emerged on the national scene as a stockbroker and editor. Among the causes she promoted were woman suffrage, spiritualism and free love, the latter a horrendous topic in the eyes of respectable people. The National leaders were impressed when she appeared before a Congressional committee on behalf of woman suffrage in 1871. For a time she basked in their favor, but her attempt to get the National's support for her presidential candidacy in 1872 threatened to disrupt the organization. Susan saved the association from this damaging influence by having the lights turned out when Mrs. Woodhull tried to address the convention.

But that was not the end of the notorious Victoria. In her paper she published the story of what she charged was a liaison between Henry Ward Beecher, probably the most famous preacher in America, and

Elizabeth Tilton, wife of Beecher's friend, Theodore Tilton. To make matters worse, Beecher had been president of the American Association, and Tilton, a prominent editor, was a friend of Susan and Mrs. Stanton. Few emerged unblemished from the scandal, although Beecher was exonerated by a church committee and his trial ended in a hung jury. Mrs. Woodhull was arrested for circulating the "obscene" story but ended up a wealthy matron in England. Poor Elizabeth Tilton saw her reputation ruined, and the suffrage movement bore the brunt of much related unfavorable publicity.

Another blow to Susan was the loss of her beloved paper. She had thrown herself into her job as manager of *The Revolution,* selling subscriptions and advertising space--but only for products that met her high standards. In Washington, she even sold a subscription to President Andrew Johnson, who yielded to get rid of this persistent saleswoman.

Susan tried to keep the paper afloat by borrowing money and adding her lecture fees to its treasury. But it was no use. Faced with mounting debts and stiff competition from the *Woman's Journal,* published by American Association members, *The Revolution* ceased publication in 1870. Susan felt as if she had lost a child and took on the obligation of the paper's $10,000 debt. When she paid the debt, after six years of lecturing, she made headlines.

In 1872, Susan put her suffrage theories to the test by voting in the presidential election. Believing that the Fourteenth and Fifteenth Amendments could be interpreted as validating suffrage for all citizens, she led a group of Rochester women to the polls, promising to pay any losses election officials suffered as a result. She was jubilant when she cast her first ballot, a straight Republican ticket, but some weeks later she was arrested for this illegal vote.

Because her attorney paid the required $1,000 bail, Susan was not able to take the case to the United States Supreme Court. Technically she was not supposed to leave Rochester, but she ignored the bothersome rule against traveling--the disapproving federal marshal often seeing her off at the station. Drumming up interest in the case, she invaded the county where the trial was to take place, speaking twenty-nine times. When the trial's location was changed, she and a friend stormed the second county.

Denouncing the law against woman suffrage, she charged: "By it, the blessings of liberty are forever withheld from women and their female posterity. To them, this government has no just powers derived from the consent of the governed. To them this government is not a democracy. It is not a republic. It is an odious aristocracy; a hateful oligarchy; the most hateful ever established on the face of the globe. . . .surely this oligarchy of sex, which makes the men of every household sovereigns, masters; the women subjects, slaves; carrying dissension, rebellion into every home of the nation, cannot be endured."

The trial of Susan B. Anthony was held in June 1873. Despite her lawyer's argument that she was being punished for an act that was commendable in a man, the judge directed the jury to present a guilty verdict. When he asked Susan if she had any comments, she was ready with a stirring protest, ending with the slogan, "Resistance to tyranny is obedience to God."

She never paid her $100 fine, nor was there any effort to collect it. The authorities must have realized that such a step would have permitted her to appeal to the Supreme Court. Although she did not win the vote, Susan did focus attention on the suffrage question, arousing considerable sympathy for the cause. Realizing the importance of this publicity, she spent $700 having a report of the trial printed and distributed. No similar action was taken against the other women voters, but the inspectors were fined and jailed. Their short stay behind bars was brightened by tempting meals sent by the women they had championed. President Grant remitted their fines, and there was a celebration at the home of Susan's sister.

Despite her sacrifice, Susan was not named among the outstanding women listed in the *Woman's Journal* around this time. Her life remained a whirl of conventions, lobbying and lecturing. When women were denied permission to present a Women's Declaration of 1876 at a centennial celebration in Philadelphia, she and several followers gained admission to the event and handed the document to the presiding official.

At a time when lectures took the place of modern mass media entertainment, Susan was a popular lecturer, as was Mrs. Stanton, who used her speaking fees to finance her children's education. Proceeds from the talks varied; Susan might average $100 a week or earn $150 for a single lecture. While she bravely discussed "Social Purity," a polite term for such taboo subjects as prostitution and sexual morality, she found it easier to speak on "Bread and the Ballot." In 1871, she traveled 13,000 miles, appearing at 170 meetings.

When suffrage referendums were scheduled, Susan would forgo more profitable lecture engagements. Her crusade took her into log cabins, sod huts and saloons, among Mormon women, and before a midnight audience on a Mississippi riverboat. In her memoirs, Mrs. Stanton recalled that just once was her friend nonplussed. That was when she was asked to speak in an insane asylum. Someone then reminded her that at last she could address an audience of her "peers"--since feminists complained that the law grouped them with lunatics and criminals in denying them the vote.

Liquor interests often opposed woman suffrage, and Susan tried to separate her cause in the public mind from that of her friend Frances E. Willard, president of the Women's Christian Temperance Union. Certain businessmen also feared the power of women voters, making it difficult to get political backing for such a contested cause. Nonpartisan in her approach, Susan accepted any support offered. There was still hostility from those who believed woman suffrage would threaten marriage and the family, and the ridicule of men and the apathy of women remained two of the heaviest crosses the feminists had to carry. Once Sioux Indians were seated in Susan's audience, innocently sporting badges that read "Against Woman Suffrage and Susan B. Anthony."

The women of Wyoming Territory had gained the right to vote in 1869. When Wyoming was ready for statehood, there was opposition in Washington to the woman suffrage provision. The feminists were apprehensive, but Wyoming decided it would not enter the Union without its women voters. But progress was slow; by 1900, women could vote in only Wyoming, Idaho, Utah and Colorado.

In the 1880's, Susan and Mrs. Stanton began the tedious task of compiling their *History of Woman Suffrage,* a work that eventually filled six volumes and was finally completed after their deaths. The first three volumes were written with the collaboration of Matilda Joslyn Gage. Susan collected all the clippings, records and documents she had been saving for years and toted them to Mrs. Stanton's New Jersey home. Poring over the mountains of material, they recorded the progress of their movement for the women who would follow. Susan and her first biographer, Ida Husted Harper, collaborated on the fourth volume and Mrs. Harper edited the subsequent books.

With the third volume, Susan took over as publisher. She gave many sets away, but recipients were not always grateful; even Harvard and Vassar initially turned down the gift. She personally directed much of the packaging and mailing of the books from the publishing headquarters in the Rochester home she shared with her sister Mary, to which she "retired" in 1891.

It was in the same decade that Susan and Lucy Stone shared a $50,000 legacy from a wealthy benefactor. The bequest helped finance Susan's publishing venture and was doubly valued since Wendell Phillips, a man she had long admired, had been involved in the proceedings. Another tribute was an $800 yearly annuity presented her on her seventy-fifth birthday, the gift of some two hundred friends.

By this time, the once reviled Susan Anthony was an international celebrity. The red shawl she wore so regularly became a symbol of the suffrage movement; on one occasion, she appeared without it and reporters refused to take notes until she put it on. She was "good copy" for the newspapers which printed such witty comments as her rebuke to a clergyman: "Doctor, your mother, if you have one, should lay you across her knee and give you a good spanking for that sermon."

Susan was one of the stars of the Chicago World's Fair of 1893 which featured a World's Congress of Representative Women. At the fair, she received a box seat and a sweeping bow from Buffalo Bill after she told some protesting ministers that a boy might profit as much from Buffalo Bill's Wild West show as from attending church on Sunday.

On her first trip to Europe in 1883, Susan had shared her dream of an international women's organization. In 1888, she greeted delegates to the International Council of Women, a gathering in Washington that marked the fortieth anniversary of the Seneca Falls event. Mrs. Stanton, away in Europe, did not want to attend, but Susan sent her an ultimatum to appear and kept a relentless eye on her old friend until she wrote her speeches.

With time slowly mending old wounds, the two factions of the suffrage movement were reunited in 1890 into the National American Woman Suffrage Association. Mrs. Stanton, who had long headed the National organization, was elected president, with Susan and Lucy Stone in other top positions. When Mrs. Stanton gave up the office two years later, Susan followed her as president.

But plump, grandmotherly Elizabeth Stanton had one more "thunderbolt" in her women's rights arsenal. It was *The Woman's Bible*, a two-volume work undertaken to set the record straight on those parts of Scripture she considered biased against women. When the National American Association denied any connection with the controversial study, Susan was angry at what she deemed a narrow-minded attitude and an insult to one who had given so much to the women's movement. She told the convention: "When our platform becomes too narrow for people of all creeds and of no creed, I myself cannot stand upon it." She was saddened when her beloved friend died in 1902.

Susan resigned as president of the National American Association in 1900, promising she would continue to "watch every potato which goes into the dinnerpot." Since the officers had never received a salary, she observed, "I retire on full pay." Her immediate successors in the office were Carrie Chapman Catt and Anna Howard Shaw.

Old age and ill health did not stop Susan. She was interested in community affairs in Rochester where she was a trustee of the State Industrial School. There she scored a minor victory for her sex by arranging that the school's laundry girls be allowed to use the more convenient washing facilities in the men's department. But she was discouraged when two girls from the school were penalized for patronizing a disreputable establishment while their male companions went free. Helping to raise the $50,000 that was the price of female admission to the University of Rochester, she pledged her own life insurance to meet the goal.

In 1903, she made her last appeal to a Senate committee, reminding the legislators that women had waited for Negroes, then for immigrants, and would next probably have to stand in line behind Filipinos, Hawaiians, Puerto Ricans and Cubans before entering the voting booth. She attended the International Council of Women assembly in Berlin in 1904 and was named honorary president of the International Woman Suffrage Alliance. In 1905, she attended the suffrage convention in Oregon, stopping in California for good measure. That same year saw her back in Washington, trying to persuade President Theodore Roosevelt to promote votes for women.

Though in poor health, she managed to appear at the Baltimore convention the next year, inspiring her audience with her belief that it was impossible for their cause to fail. She died two months later, March 13, 1906, at the age of eighty-six. Fourteen years later, a century after her birth, American women were finally granted the right to vote. They have made great strides since then, but today they still clamor for "equal rights" in the struggle that is the legacy of Susan B. Anthony.

BIBLIOGRAPHY

Adams, Mildred. *The Right to Be People*. Philadelphia: Lippincott, 1967.

Anthony, Katharine. *Susan B. Anthony: Her Personal History and Her Era*. Garden City, N.Y.: Doubleday, 1954.

Burnett, Constance Buel. *Five for Freedom*. New York: Abelard Press, 1953.

Catt, Carrie Chapman, and Nettie Roger Shuler. *Woman Suffrage and Politics: The Inner Story of the Suffrage Movement*. New York: C. Scribner's Sons, 1923.

Flexner, Eleanor. *Century of Struggle: The Woman's Rights Movement in the United States*. Cambridge, Mass.: Harvard University Press, 1959.

Gattey, Charles Nelson. *The Bloomer Girls*. New York: Coward-McCann, 1968.

Harper, Ida Husted. *The Life and Work of Susan B. Anthony* (three volumes). Indianapolis: Hollenbeck, 1898, 1908. (Available in an Arno Press Inc. reprint, 1969.)

Hays, Elinor Rice. *Morning Star: A Biography of Lucy Stone, 1818-1893*. New York: Harcourt, Brace and World, 1961.

Johnston, Johanna. *Mrs. Satan: The Incredible Saga of Victoria C. Woodhull*. New York: G.P. Putnam's Sons, 1967.

Lutz, Alma. *Created Equal: A Biography of Elizabeth Cady Stanton, 1815-1902*. New York: John Day, 1940.

—————————. *Crusade for Freedom. Women in the Antislavery Movement*. Boston: Beacon Press, 1968.

—————————. *Susan B. Anthony: Rebel, Crusader, Humanitarian*. Boston: Beacon Press, 1959.

O'Neill, William L. *Everyone Was Brave: The Rise and Fall of Feminism in America*. Chicago: Quadrangle Books, 1969.

Riegel, Robert E. *American Feminists*. Lawrence, Kans.: University of Kansas Press, 1963.

—————————. *American Women: A Story of Social Change*. Rutherford, N.J.: Fairleigh Dickinson University Press, 1970.

Sinclair, Andrew. *The Better Half: The Emancipation of the American Woman*. New York: Harper and Row, 1965.

Smith, Page. *Daughters of the Promised Land: Women in American History*. Boston: Little, Brown, 1970.

Stanton, Elizabeth Cady. *Eighty Years and More: Reminiscences 1815-1897*. Reprinted by Source Book Press, New York, 1970, and Schocken Books, New York, 1971, from the T. Fisher Unwin edition of 1898.

Stanton, Elizabeth Cady, Susan B. Anthony, Matilda Joslyn Gage, and Ida Husted Harper, editors. *History of Woman Suffrage* (six volumes). New York and Rochester: Fowler and Wells; Susan B. Anthony; National American Woman Suffrage Association, 1881-1922. (Available in an Arno Press Inc. reprint, 1969.)

Stanton, Theodore, and Harriot Stanton Blatch, editors. *Elizabeth Cady Stanton As Revealed in Her Letters, Diary and Reminiscences* (two volumes). Reprinted by Arno Press Inc., New York, 1969, from the Harper and Brothers edition, 1922.

SamHar Press

Division of Story House Corp.